Franklin Carr

Twenty-two Years in State Prisons

Franklin Carr

Twenty-two Years in State Prisons

ISBN/EAN: 9783744758840

Printed in Europe, USA, Canada, Australia, Japan

Cover: Foto ©ninafisch / pixelio.de

More available books at **www.hansebooks.com**

State Prisons

By FRANKLIN CARR.

PHILADELPHIA.

1893.

INTRODUCTION.

The author of this little book has asked me to write an introductory word. It must be but a word. Its pages tell a tenderly pathetic story of sorrow, sin and salvation. They show how a child, not naturally worse than other children, may be made worse by parental indifference. They teach that home is the best "House of Refuge," and that reformatory institutions, so-called, are sometimes little better than nurseries of crime. They indicate that courtesy and kindness, and not curses and kicks, are the better methods of reforming criminals. They bring a message of hope to the worst of men; showing that the vilest and most sinful may be saved if they will but turn to Christ. And last, though not least, they show that the humble and obscure, as well as the cultured and prominent, may be made of God the honored instruments in winning souls to Christ. May the blessing of God ever rest upon the author and accompany the reading of his sadly eventful life.

Yours in gospel bonds,

REV. JOSEPH B. GRAFF.

M. E. Parsonage, No. 2039 E. York St., Philadelphia, Pa.
January 5, 1893.

TWENTY-TWO YEARS

IN

STATE PRISONS.

I, Franklin Carr, better known as "Big Frank," was born in New York city on the 16th of February, 1846. We moved to Philadelphia, Pa., about one year after I was born, where my father was killed on a railroad and brought home dead. Of course I was too young to realize my loss, and my mother was left a widow with me, her only child, to care for. She tried to raise me up to be a good Christian and to love God, who could be a husband to the widow and a father to the orphan, but it seemed that I was born to get into all kinds of scrapes, for I got what is known as a step-father, and he did not believe in God or the Devil. He did not believe much in me, and so my life began to be a miserable one. My mother would dress me up nice and clean and send me out to play, and would say, "Now, Frankie, be a good boy and don't get your clothes dirty," and I would say, "yes, ma'am," but as soon as I got off out of her sight I would forget all about my promises and I would go after the 'busses and wagons and fall off in the mud in the street and get my clothes all dirty and torn, and then my step-father would knock me down and beat me unmercifully. I started out with some other boys to dig a cave, and we were to play robbers, but before the cave was dug I came to grief. I was moving my little foot along to show another boy where to chop the ground with a hatchet, but my toe was so full of the same kind of dirt that he took it for the ground, and down came the hatchet on my toe. The other little fellow took his hat in one hand and away he went; I almost can see that boy run now as I write this narrative.

Well, that stopped my play for quite awhile to come. My step-father found a school that I could go to for the small amount of ten cents a week. The school met in a vacant store, and we had two teachers, man and wife; but I never heard anything like a lesson while I was there. The principal exercises consisted in laughing at the teachers whipping the little girls over the lower limbs with the cat-o'nine-tails, and in asking permission to go home and get a piece of bread and molasses. And so it went on until the schoolmaster and mistress came to the school one day so drunk that they could not open the door. Then the parents of the children would not send their children there any more, and that ended my schooling until I was six years old, when I was sent to a public school. The first day I went to that school some boy had thrown a spit ball or something of that sort, and he had the fun while I got the whipping, and the consequence was the teacher and I had a fight. She used the rattan while I used the slate, and I came out the victor; but I had to fight another one when I got home, and the enemy (my step-father, who was a powerful man) being much stronger, of course I was badly whipped and was laid up for two weeks from the effects. My mother was absent at the time on a visit to the country. When she came home I told her all about it, and that made him so angry that he kicked me out into the street. The neighbors were afraid to take me in, so I had to sleep in a butcher's wagon in a slaughter house and sometimes in packing boxes. My mother used to bring me in the house when he was away and give me food and money, and after three or four months my step-father bound me out with a farmer in Montgomery county, who treated me very badly. He would get me out of bed when the stars were shining in the morning and keep me working as long as I could at night, and his wife used to pull my hair and shake me so that I got afraid to go near her.

Everything her own children did they would blame on me, and she was only too willing to believe them. It went on in this way till I could stand it no longer, and then I ran away from them and came back to the city.

A short time after this, when I was about seven years of age, my mother died. She told them to bring me to her, and as I remember standing there at the deathbed of my mother, the only friend I had in the world passing away from me, I was so dazed I could neither speak, cry nor do anything else. I could hardly realize my loss; it was all I could do to understand what she was saying to me. I remember her telling me to be a good boy and God would take care of me. My step-father and a number of others were standing around the bed, and as she turned her eyes toward them and said, "Remember my boy Frank, and take care of him, and bring him up in the way he should go," they promised her they would; but they soon forgot their promises. Some four or five weeks after my mother died they placed me in a House of Refuge or a Reform School. The Superintendent took me by the hand, and seating himself alongside of me, talked very kindly, and told me to tell him something about my life, and said he would be my friend. He turned out to be a true friend to me, and I was placed in the brush shop to work. I was made office boy shortly after that, where I received more privilege than most of the boys; but I found the House of Refuge was only a school for crime. When a new boy was turned in the yard among four or five hundred other boys, they would get around him and ask him what he was in there for, and when he would tell them that he was put there by his father, or mother, or guardians, they would laugh and say, "Is that all?" Of course, it would be natural for him to ask them the same question, and one would tell how he tapped a till, or, in other words, robbed a money drawer, and would show all about how it was done. Another would tell how he picked pockets; how he had been brought up in a school for young pickpockets; and another would tell how his father or brother were crooked men, or, in other words, were burglars, and had used him for transom work; so that a boy would learn more there in one month than he would in five years outside. That was the first place I ever learned to pick a lock. We used to pick the locks of the officers' rooms to steal tobacco from; or if a boy got locked up for punishment we would unlock his door and let him out again.

I was at the House of Refuge for a period of three years. When I was released I found my step-father had married my mother's sister. After I went home they treated me very badly. My step-father knocked me down and jumped on me until I was bruised so badly I

had to be put to bed. Shortly after that I was returned
to the House of Refuge again, where I spent two years
and a half more. When I left there again I was home-
less and friendless; nowhere to go, no one to help me,
and the only situation that would afford me a home was
to tend a bar in a gambling saloon, one of the worst at
that time in the city of Philadelphia. There I became
acquainted with thieves and gamblers. We never
closed that place day or night, and as there was no
Sunday liquor law at that time, of course the place was
never closed. We had a private entrance "for ladies,"
at least that is what the sign read over the door on the
outside. There was a bell rope in every room that rang
a bell behind the bar, so that we could tell what room
they were in. I have seen young girls from sixteen to
eighteen years old, and some that even looked younger
than that, with their hair down over their faces, and so
drunk that they had to be taken to their homes in a
hack early in the morning. And then we had in the back
part, what is known in bar-rooms as a card room, where
young men could sit down and gamble for drinks and
money, and some of those young men were from fifteen to eighteen years old, and about as bright a set of
boys as you would meet anywhere; but they soon began to show that dissipated and don't-care look. I
remember one boy that used to come there by the name

of Harry White. A bright little fellow he was, with rosy cheeks, and a smile for every one. He would come in with his Sunday school books on a Sunday morning, when his parents thought he was in the Sabbath school, and he would say, " Frank, is Sunday school commenced?" and I would answer, "Yes; they are up stairs in No. 5 room waiting for their teacher to come," and there they would sit all day on the Sabbath playing cards and drinking whiskey. In order to do this they had to have money, and some of them would tell their mother or father that they got less wages than they really did get, so that they deceived their parents; and some of them would take small amounts of money from time to time from their employers. And many times have I had their parents, either a poor old father or mother, almost broken-hearted, come looking for their boy, and they would say, " Has my boy been here to-night?" and I would answer, " No; I have not seen him to-night," when I knew it was a lie ; but I had to lie or lose my place. The boy would probably be lying in the back room at the time so drunk that he could not get off the chair, or, if lying on the floor, he would not be able to stand upon his feet. I have taken them home and put them on the steps, and then rung the bell, and left them there to be taken in by their parents. Of those boys who used to meet in that saloon at that time one of them died in the insane asylum; another died with the delirium tremens, and one committed suicide by jumping out of a window while having the delirium tremens; another died with consumption brought on by exposure, and two of them went to State Prison.

I remember one Sunday morning Mr. White was standing at the bar when his son Harry stepped in, and as he came near the bar he caught sight of his father. They stood like two statues looking at each other. At last Mr. White spoke, and the first words he said were, " How long have you been coming here, my boy?" And the son put on a saucy look and answered with a toss of his curly head, "How long have you been coming here?" Mr. White did not get angry, but as he looked at his son I saw tears flowing down his cheeks. He called his son aside, and they had a long talk together. At last the father took his son's hand and they went out together, and I never saw father or son in that saloon again.

There was one young man who used to come to that saloon by the name of Willie Myers. I knew him when I was a little fellow going to school, and I remember when he went to learn his trade at brass finishing. He came into that saloon one day and looked all around to see if any one knew him, and when he saw that no one knew him he stepped up to the bar and called for a glass of whiskey. After drinking it he commenced coughing and strangling, while the tears ran down his cheeks. He said, "That is good whiskey." I said, " Yes, we don't keep anything but the best of everything here." I knew that he was no judge of anything. The next time he came in he didn't seem to mind who was there so much, and after awhile one glass was not enough; he wanted more. He married a young girl I also knew when going to school, and when they were married they were as happy a couple as ever you would wish to see. They had a nice little house furnished from top to bottom, but rum broke it up. Some years after this his wife came to me on a cold winter's night. She had a shawl wrapped around her head and she said, "Frank, I want you to come with me quick." When we got to the house I found that they lived in an attic. She took a candle to light me up the stairs, and when we got in the room I looked around, and instead of the fine furniture, I found there an old bedstead tied up with ropes to keep it from falling, one chair and a block of wood for seats, a little round stove and just a square pine table, and that was all the furniture there was in the room. Lying on the bed was a young man in delirium tremens, and two men (one his brother) were holding him down. His wife, pointing to the bed, said, "*Frank*, there is your work; *you* made *him* what he is." That was a scene I never could erase from my memory. I would cut off my right arm now rather than sell another glass of rum over the bar to man, woman or child.

We had on the second floor of that saloon a gambling room. I remember one old gentleman with long white hair, over eighty years of age, and who was worth considerable property. His poor old wife, who was aged and infirm, used to stand outside and cry and wring her hands, waiting for him to come out; but he never would go out till he had lost every dollar that he carried. I do not know what became of him afterwards. That is one of the many cases that I have seen ruined in the gambling saloon. A gambler is no more or less than a thief. He will rob you of every cent that you own. If he allows you to win ten or fifteen dollars he has a purpose for doing so; but if he thinks there is no more to be got from you he will not allow you to win anything. They will tell you that faro bank is the fairest game there is with cards, but there is a certain working of that little silver box whereby a professional gambler can draw out a red or black card as he pleases. So you can see that you have not a ghost of a chance with a professional gambler. Most all gamblers I ever knew learned playing cards at home; just a social little game for pastime. Then they would play for pennies to make it interesting, and from that went to gambling for a living.

That was the first I got acquainted with gamblers and
thieves. There was one in particular that I took a great
fancy to. He was a great man in my eyes. They called
him "Captain." He said he would make a good man
out of me, and told me some great yarns that I would
have plenty of good clothes, plenty of money and a
good time of it, and when he took me away from there
one evening he took me to a house in the lower sec-
tion of the city where he said I would have a good
time and the boys would like me; but when I got there
that house fell in my estimation considerably. Instead
of them liking me they got to fighting over me. It was
a small square room with a small table in the middle of
the floor, and a lot of men sitting around playing cards,
and a girl sixteen or seventeen years of age filling up the
glasses with liquor for them to drink. As we came
through the door they jumped to their feet and wanted
to know what he brought that boy there for, and they
soon got to fighting with knives. As I saw the glim-
mer of the knives in the glare of the lamp I was very
much frightened; boy-like, I shrank off in a corner for I
was not so hardened in sin as I afterwards became. The
captain told them to let me alone; I had the right stuff in
me and I would make a good man. So the girl that was
waiting on them got them quiet again, and one of them
took hold of me by the collar and pointing a revolver in

my face said he wanted me to listen to him; he said if I
would ever "squeal" on them in any way he would shoot
me like a dog.   Then he told me to take my seat and
offered me a glass of whiskey; I told him I did not
want it.   But he made me drink it, "for," he said, "you
will want it before morning."   About midnight one of
them said, "Well, Jim, get the tools ready and let us get
to work."

I wondered what kind of work they did at that hour
of the night, but I was not kept long in ignorance.   They
brought the tools out and looked them over, and then
they asked if he had the jimmy nipps, and if they had
the lanterns and drills, and a number of other tools too
numerous to mention.   When they were ready they
buttoned up my overcoat and wrapped a scarf around
my neck and we were soon on our way out of the city
on the cars.   That was my first lesson in the art of a
cracksman or a burglar.

We went into a small town up the State and were
robbing a mansion, when some one coming home late
gave the alarm.   That was the first time I knew what it
was to have a howling mob after us.   A lot of farmers
got after us with lanterns, shot guns and pitchforks; it
was after a hard rain and the roads were full of mud.   I
ran till I was exhausted and covered with mud and could
run no longer.   I was so frightened I threw myself down

by a fence in a corner and for some reason or other they passed me by and went after the men. The next morning when I got back into the city I was in a sorry plight, and had anybody taken an interest in me I believe it would have been my last step in crime; but I was left to myself and soon got as bad as the rest of them, so much so that I had to leave the city and go West. I went out into the State of Ohio where I got in with a gang of crooks as bad as any I had left behind in Philadelphia. There I changed my name and went under the name of Bill Pool. I now began to study the business as a profession, and was soon known as one of the worst in the State. I had joined a gang known as the " Bell Boys." There were three of them in the penitentiary at that time, and a woman who kept what is known among crooks as a "fence" furnished me with a set of burglars' tools, and I soon became a terror to that State. I had robbed a place up at McCoy station and then cut a boat loose on the river and rowed down to Steubenville. Then I set the boat adrift and took the steamboat Othello, on my way to Wheeling, West Virginia, to commit a crime, but before we got there the boat was hailed at Martin's Ferry where the authorities came aboard and put my partner (a young man by the name of John Hamilton) and me in irons. We were taken, by rail, back to Steubenville. I waived a hearing at the time so I could hear from my friend and get counsel. Two days after I was bound over in $2000 bail to appear at court, and when I came up for trial I was four days getting tried. The sheriff spoke a good word for me and said I had behaved like a gentleman while under his charge in the jail, and when the judge told me to stand up for sentence he said, "I could give you ten years, but your counsel has pleaded so earnestly, and the sheriff has spoken so well of you, that I will give you five years in the Ohio penitentiary where you will find that the way of the transgressor is hard."

It was announced in the papers that we would be taken to the penitentiary the next day, but we were not taken for two or three days after. When I got out of there I met the sheriff again, and he said he did not expect to get us there without a good deal of trouble, for he thought some of the gang would attack the train somewhere along the road, and that was the reason we did not go up as advertised.

When I got in that prison I did find that the way of the transgressor was hard. They took me into one of the cell-houses, and there we found a guard who told us to take a seat. I tried to speak to him, but he told me to keep my mouth shut until I was spoken to. Then he took a card from his desk about two feet long and about ten inches wide, and when he read it to me I found

I was not to talk, laugh, wink, look at visitors or the other prisoners, or do anything but what I was told to do. I found that the least infringement of these rules brought a ducking in the tub until one was almost drowned. I was taken from the cell-house to the bath-room and put under the shower bath, and my own clothes taken away and a striped convict suit handed to me to put on. Then I was marched over to the chapel, which was called the idle room, where we had to sit in rows through the week, and were not allowed to speak a word to those along-side of us. There was a guard to watch us that we should not talk, and woe unto the one that was caught moving his lips.

The next day I was placed in one of the foundries to work. I was marched up in company with about thirty-five other men in lock step, with the right hand on the shoulder of the man in front of me. We all had to keep our faces turned to the left so the guard could see if we talked, and they would shout, "Don't let me see daylight between you." When the first bell would ring the company would all march up into the yard, and at the second bell we would march into the dining-room and stand in front of our places until the third bell, when we would take our seats. Then they would ring a small bell in the dining-room when we would take off our caps and the chaplain would say grace. I looked at

the food, but could not eat any; it consisted of a piece of
corn bread, a bowl of water and a spoonful of hominy.
I saw that the man next to me looked hungry enough
to eat it, but I could not say, "You can have it," without
first raising my hand, which I did. Then the guard
came down to me and wanted to know what I wanted,
and when I asked him if I could give my dinner to the
man next to me, he said yes, but that I had better eat
my own dinner. I told him that I could not; and then
I could not say, "you can have this dinner;" all I could
do was to push it over to him. I wish some of my
readers could have seen that man eat the dinner. It was
gone before I thought he had time to commence; I found
I could eat it, too, before I got out, for we did not get
half enough to eat, such as it was. I have seen men sit
down in the foundry and cry because they were tasked so
hard and were so hungry that they could not do their task,
and I said if I ever live to get out of here I will never get
in prison again; but when I got out of prison I never
found any Christian who would take me by the hand and
say, "Frank, come, go along with me and I will show
you a better way to live," or, "we will get you a situation
so that you can earn an honest living." But the devil
always had his agents outside to wait for me, and they
would say, "Well, Frank, old boy; I am glad to see you
out again. Let's go over and have something," and

"something" always meant a glass of whiskey. Then I would drift back into the old life of sin and crime.

The prison in which I was confined is built on the Scioto river, at Columbus, Ohio. When I got out of it (there were seven of us released the same morning, and two companions that I met outside, making nine of us all together) we went over to a Columbus saloon and had a drink, and then bought some things to send to the prisoners inside, such as handkerchiefs, tobacco, etc. Then we went and bought our tickets for Cincinnati, and as we had plenty of rum on board we soon got in high spirits and came near having a fight before we got there. After we got to Cincinnati we split up and I and my companions crossed the Ohio river to Newport, Kentucky, and from there we went to Louisville, Kentucky. We stayed there about a week, going to the theaters, gambling and committing all kinds of crime. Then we crossed the river to Jeffersonville, Indiana, and visited the State Prison, and then on to Indianapolis, where I met a young man who gave me a tract and invited me up to a meeting of the Young Men's Christian Association. I said I would go if he would go with me. "All right, Frank," he said, "I will go with you." I was so astonished to hear him call me by name, I asked him if he knew who I was. He said, "yes." Then he had a long talk with me, and asked me to promise not to steal any more. I told him I would not promise him. He said he did not want me to promise him but to promise God. I told him I would promise him I would not steal anything in Indianapolis, and I kept my word, for I never did rob a place in that town.

I went from there to Terra Haute, Indiana, and from there to St. Louis, committing crimes all the time. I took a ramble around the city; around Christy avenue and the vilest portions. Then I went up to the "four courts," then along the levee and visited some of the worst dives that can be found in any city. They were called the "Blazing Stump," the "Hole in the Wall," and such names. I will try to describe one of them called the "Blazing Stump." When I went in at the door all eyes were turned on me. One dirty looking individual put his hand on my shoulder and said, "Say, pard, ain't you going to treat?" I shook his hand from my shoulder and told him not to get so familiar; I then called all hands up to the bar and treated them, and then had a chance to look around me. There was a dirty looking man and a boy behind the bar, and I think there was a woman there, too. The floor was black with dirt; it looked as if it had never been scrubbed. Afterwards I turned my attention to those around me, and found the hardest looking lot I ever met. There were 'longshoremen who unload the steamboats, and bums and tramps, and petty sneak thieves. There were black and white men, and there were some that looked as if they had seen better days. Some were literally covered with vermin. The customers could get a bowl of soup and a piece of bread for the small sum of five cents, and they had all kinds of things to sell that they either stole or begged somewhere. One would say, " Cap, don't you want to buy a good coat, or pants or vest?" and another would have a ring or a watch to sell that had been stolen somewhere, and I noticed that while I was there a policeman looked in several times as though he was looking for some one. I treated again and then went out, for the smell of the place made me sick. I went up to the hotel and had something to eat, and the next day I was so sick I thought I would die. I found that everybody avoided me, and I did not know what was the matter, so I went to see a doctor. He looked at me as if I was some ghost that came to haunt him, and told me to go up to the guardians of the poor. I went there and the doctor talked very kindly to me and asked me how I felt. Then he took me through a window onto a porch and told me to sit there until he came to see me again; and he kept me there from about ten o'clock in the morning until about half-past three in the afternoon. When he came to me again he asked me how I felt, and I told him that I did not feel any better for sitting there; and he said, "I suppose not, but you have all the symptoms of small pox." I told him I hadn't the small pox, and he said, "I know you have not now." In a few minutes I was put in an ambulance and taken to the depot and put on a train and sent to Carondelet to the City Hospital, where I was treated very kindly. I found that I had the ague and intermittent fever and came very near dying that time; but I got so tired of the hospital that I came out before I was well, although the doctor tried to persuade me to stay until I got a little stronger.

I came back to St. Louis from the hospital and visited what is known as the Soup House. I had heard so much about it in the hospital, I was anxious to see it. It was situated in the neighborhood of Eleventh and Chestnut streets, and when I got there I found it had been a large tobacco warehouse. A policeman was standing at the door and I asked him if I could go in and see the place. He very kindly took me in to show me around. The first thing I saw was a square-shaped place boarded off, something like a counter, and behind it were a number of ladies with a lot of soup boilers. They were handing soup in large tin cups to the men. I noticed also along the walls were wooden bunks for the men to lay in at night, row on top of row. After staying there awhile and looking around, I thanked them very kindly and bid them good-bye. That night I went to Jack

Rooney's variety show and after drinking plenty of beer
and whiskey, I went back to the hotel.

The next day I took passage for New Orleans. While
on the boat I made a new acquaintance, a very flashily
dressed young man who seemed very attentive to me.
He asked me to have a cigar and then commenced to ask
me a great many questions as to where I came from, and
invited me to take a drink down in the saloon. After
drinking he asked me over to see them play cards. Then
he asked me if I would like to take a hand that we might
win some money. I saw into the game right away; I
saw that they were all in one ring. I told them I did not
know much about playing cards but would take a hand
in it. I had not forgotten the old trade I had learned
while tending bar in a Philadelphia gambling saloon.
The consequence was I came out of that game with over
$500. I got up and walked over to the other end of the
boat and sat down by myself, thinking over my past life
and wondering what it would come to. When I landed
in New Orleans I went up Canal street and went into a
gambling saloon where I lost about $25. I then went
around to the French market and got something to eat;
then back to the gambling saloon again, and when I left
there that night I was over $200 ahead. As I was leav-
ing the place a young man tapped me on the shoulder
(it was the young man I met on the steamboat) and

asked me to take a walk around town. I felt in my pocket to see if my revolver was all right. He noticed the motion and smiled and told me I had no use for that. After we got outside he said, "who in the world are you, anyhow?" I told him I was only a stranger, looking at the sights and to see the "elephant." After strolling around that night we went to a hotel to sleep. From that time we became fast friends.

I now commenced my life as a gambler on the Mississippi river, making St. Louis my headquarters. We would gamble from St. Louis to Memphis, Cairo and New Orleans, and back again. I kept up this life for some time until I was run off the boat as a gambler and a blackleg, and as a nuisance generally. Then I went to gambling on the railroad, going up one road and down another until we were run off the railroads.

One day while walking out Carondelet avenue I met two friends who said they had a job up the State and wanted me to help them. We went up the State of Missouri about two hundred miles, and came very near never coming back again, for we were caught by a vigilance committee and came very near being lynched. In fact, we would have been if it had not been for the sheriff who rescued us from mob law by gathering a posse of deputies. Then they put us in jail and placed a strong guard around us, not that they were afraid we

VILLAGE SCENE

would escape, but that they wanted to keep them from molesting us. When we were brought up in court the judge gave us five years in the Missouri State Penitentiary. The prison was built upon a high bluff alongside of Jefferson City; and below the prison was the quarry. Below that was the Missouri Pacific railroad, along which the guards were stationed, armed with guns, to see that we did not escape. Below the railroad ran the Missouri river, the swiftest river in the world, which would carry a man ten or twelve miles down stream before he could reach the other side. I came to the conclusion that I would have to stay my time out in that prison. In addition to the force already mentioned, any citizen would arrest a convict who tried to escape, hunting him down with dogs and guns, and he would be well nigh perished when brought back. When I entered the prison they asked me what I did for a living. I did not like to say I did nothing but steal, so I told them I was a bartender. They said I was just the man they wanted to tend bar. I did not know what they meant at the time, but the next day he put me in the quarry, and put a large iron crowbar in my hand, and told me to attend to that. Not being used to that kind of a bar, I soon had my hands full of blisters.

When I got out of that prison I went away with the intention of doing better. I thought as I had not made

3

a good citizen I would perhaps make a better soldier, so I went to Leavenworth, Kansas, and enlisted in the regular army. I was sent from there to Fort Larned, and I found that the devil was just as strong in the army as in citizen life, for I was in the guard house most of my time for being drunk and fighting. One day I went on a pass to a town seven miles and a half from the fort, and staying over my pass, was put in the guard house for absence without leave. The next morning at guard mount, when the officer of the day called my name, I did not answer quickly enough to suit him, so he struck me with his sword and called me a name I would not take from any man at that time, and the consequence was I knocked him down for it, and was court martialed and sentenced to carry a thirty-six pound ball and a six foot chain riveted to the left ankle for three years. General Pope reduced the term to one year, and I carried that ball two months before court martialed and one year afterward. I had to work with it from sunrise to sunset, in the hot sun, and sleep with it all night; had to cut wood for the officers' quarters, and when they didn't want any wood cut I had to dig a hole and then turn around and fill it up again. After serving my term in the guard house (I was then in Fort Dodge with my company) I was discharged for disability.

I then went to Denver, Colorado, and joined a gang of

gamblers and desperadoes. I went from there over the
Denver Pacific to Cheyenne and stayed there awhile,
gambling and stealing. I then went over towards Fort
Fetterman, and came very near being caught for stealing
horses by the Vigilance Committee. I then came back
to Cheyenne and took the Union Pacific railroad to
Ogden. I then took a trip down into Salt Lake City to
pay the Mormons a visit, and while there I went up to
Camp Jackson to see the soldiers. The fort is built on a
bluff a short distance outside of the city. After staying
there a few days I came back to Ogden. Then I went to
San Francisco, Cal. I stayed there quite a while and
went out as far as La Pass Louer, Cal, I visited several
places, Oakland, Brooklyn, San Sylito and Sacramento,
and other towns too numerous to mention. I afterwards
left there and came East as far as Omaha, Nebraska. I
afterwards went West to Sydney, Nebraska, where I
enlisted again in the regular army, where we had to
escort bull trains from Sydney to *fort* Red Cloud
Agency. After a few months of that kind of duty we
were shipped on a train to Medicine Bow, where we met
some more troops, and, after camping there two days,
went to Fort Fetterman, where we met some more troops
on the North Platte river. After camping there awhile
the government gave us seal skin caps, gloves and arctic
shoes, the weather was so severe. Then we were

marched from there to Fort Reno, on the Powder River. After camping outside the fort for a few days we were paid off, and the soldiers spent all their time in gambling. After we left there we had a hard time of it. Our rations ran out and they could get none up to us. We had a supply camp at Crazy Woman's Fork. We were marched up into the Big Horn mountains. While there we had a fight with the Indians, and that is where I lost my finger. After marching around that country from November until February, the weather was so severe that we were ordered in. We came into Camp Carlon, just outside of Cheyenne, where they put us on a train over the Denver Pacific road. When we got to Denver the train was side-tracked, and we laid there all night. The next morning we were sent over the Kansas Pacific road, and at some of the watering places the plugs were frozen up, so we had to lay over for hours trying to get water for the engines. When we got to Fort Leavenworth it was about midnight, and we were a sorry looking lot of men. One of the companies that was stationed there furnished us with hot coffee. After that I was discharged from the army again. In a little while I was sentenced for three years in the Kansas State Penitentiary.

After leaving that prison I was determined to reform, so I went back to Philadelphia. Had any one taken me in hand I would have been changed, for I was tired of the life I was leading and was willing enough to give it up; but I did not know how to go about it. I did not think Jesus would have anything to do with men like me that had led such wicked lives, so I went down again among my old companions, where I was sure of a welcome. They gave me a shake of the hand, asked me how things were out West, and told me they were glad to see me again, as they had a job to do up the State. When I told them I had given up the business and intended to lead a better life, they said I felt out of sorts ; to take a good drink and I would be all right. I did so, and guess I must have got crazy, for liquor always made me wild. We went up in the coal regions and committed several burglaries until we reached Scranton, Pa. We robbed a place, and no one saw us but God, but it seems that I left an impression on paper of my left hand (the hand from which the finger was lost) and the detectives knew who committed that crime. The papers published the facts and I was caught. If you had been there the morning I was brought back on the cars, you would have thought it was a holiday. What was it for? To see a poor man driven along the streets with handcuffs on his hands. The policemen threatened to club me for telling the people to get out of the way so I could walk.

After they took my photograph they put me in jail,

and, after two months' time, I was sentenced to solitary confinement at hard labor for seven years. As I had a good deal of the devil in me, and would not work, I was often put on bread and water and confined in a cell with nothing but the bare floor to sleep on. After my release I got a situation on the Philadelphia and Reading railroad, and served the company faithfully. One day, after I came in from a trip, I was told to report at the office. I could not think of anything wrong I had done, but when I went in the office they told me my services were no longer required. When I asked the reason they would give me none; but some time afterwards I learned that detectives had gone there and told them they had an ex-convict in their employ.

Then I got a place on Arch street to work and got along pretty well. This man trusted me to collect bills, pay bills, and sometimes buy goods. One day when I came in the son told me his father wanted me in his private office. When I went in he turned the key in the door and told me to sit down. Then he said I was no longer needed. I asked for a reason, and he said as far as my work went I had done as well as any one he ever had, but he heard something that day of my past life, and he had no further use for such a man as I had been.

Well, I did not know what to do. The devil told me

respectable people did not want such as me around them and it was no use trying any more. So I went to the rum shop to drown my sorrow. I got drunk and went down to my old companions. "Ah!" they said, "Frank, we knew you would be back again, for those Christian hypocrites and long-faces do not want anything to do with us except to put us in prison."

I believed what they said, for it seemed only too true from what I had seen of them, and it was not long before I was sent back to the Eastern Penitentiary for two years more, along with another young man whom I had known for years. Most of those last two years I laid on the sick-bed with hemorrhages of the lungs, never expecting to get out of there alive.

When I got out, in the middle of winter, hardly able to walk, I met two of my old chums outside of the gate who knew that my time would be up that morning, and had come out to meet me, and they said, "Well, Frank, old boy; we are glad to see you out again, but you look as if you came out of a graveyard." So they asked me over to take a drink, and when I told them I did not want it, they said it would be the best medicine I could take for a man as sick as I was. So I went with them, and the first day out of prison I got drunk again, as sick as I was. I had promised to meet them the next day, but before I could meet them I was standing on the corner of Eighth and Vine streets, where I met a young man by the name of William H. Evans, who had been a Christian for some time.

So ends the dark side of my life.

The Bright Side of Life.

This young man, whom I met at the corner of Eighth and Vine streets, by the name of William H. Evans, was a Christian. He took me by the hand and said he was glad to see me, and asked me to go with him. He said his wife would be glad to see me, as she had not seen me for some time. I tried to put him off, saying I had to meet a couple of friends; but he insisted that I should go with him, saying that those kind of friends were never any good to me. At last I consented to go with him. After we had dinner and sat talking awhile, I said, Well, good-bye, Willie; I will come and see you again. He asked me where I was going, and I told him I thought I would go up to Eighth and Vine a little while. He said he would take a walk up that way with me.

So we started out together, and he never lost sight of me until evening. Then he said I had better go and take supper with him, but I told him I would sooner go and take supper with my old friend, Mr. John A. Clayton, who had been more than a brother to me; he was my little playmate when I was six years of age, and who stuck to me when everybody else seemed to turn their backs on me. When I was in prison he would write to me and bring me anything that I was allowed to have, and I have lived with him ever since I have been out of prison. But Willie said I was too weak to walk down there for supper, and that I had better go and take supper with him.

After we had supper I bade him good-night, and he said, " Where are you going to-night? " I said I thought I would go to one of the theatres, so he said he would take a walk up that way with me. We walked about in the neighborhood of Eighth and Vine streets until we heard singing at a corner that used to be a saloon when I went to prison. It had since been converted into a mission. Willie Evans said to me: " Let us go in there awhile and hear them sing, and we can rest ourselves." We sat right in front of the superintendent, whose name was James Johnson, or, as they called him, Jimmy Johnson. He was telling how thieves and drunkards had been saved in the Jerry McAuley Mission in New York city, and I thought to myself, Can this be true that such bad men had been saved? It seemed to me that he was talking directly to me; and when they gave the

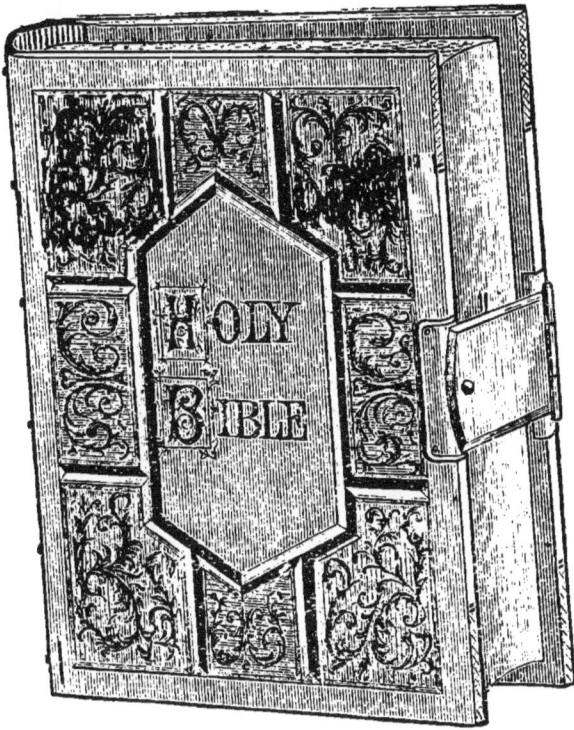

invitation to raise the hand for the prayers of those good people, I looked around me and saw that those people had what I did not have, and I felt I would like to live a better life, if I could.

Willie told me to raise my hand, and I told him it was no use for me to do so. He told me it would do me no harm if it did no good, and then I raised my hand. It was not long before two or three of them got around me and told me that Jesus loved me; and I told them that they did not know how bad I had been. Then they told me it did not make any difference how bad I had been, and one lady invited me to go into the inquiry room. After a little hesitation, I got up and walked back in the room, and she talked to me and told me about Jesus and the story of the cross, and how He saved the thief in the last hour; and she told me what He did for the thief over eighteen hundred years ago He could do for the thief to-day. She said a good many other things about Jesus that I do not remember just now, but she told me to get on my knees and pray that Jesus would save me. I said I do not know how to pray, and then she said, "I will teach you how to pray." I stayed on my knees until nearly twelve o'clock that night, and then I went to the place where I was stopping and got on my knees again and stayed there until between two and three o'clock in the morning, when

I felt as if a heavy burden had rolled 'off of me, and I felt like shouting for joy, for I knew that the Lord had heard my cry for mercy.

That was two years ago, and the Lord has taken care of me ever since. I have been going about from one church to another, and from one mission to another, telling what a wonderful Saviour I have found and speaking to those that were down in the gutter of sin and crime where I myself had been. I have known men to raise their hands for prayer just to get into the inquiry room to coax me out to take a drink, and they have even stood outside of the door and poked a bottle of whiskey under my nose to tempt me back into the world again, and I have had the detectives follow me around day after day, and at last they arrested me for robbing a safe on Arch street that I did not know anything about, but God raised up good friends for me and brought me through all right, for I knew it would be easy to sentence me on my previous bad character and circumstantial evidence.

Since I have been preaching and telling others the story of the cross, the Lord has blessed me wonderfully.

I remain, your brother in Christ,

FRANKLIN CARR.

Philadelphia, Pa., January 5, 1893.

www.ingramcontent.com/pod-product-compliance
Lightning Source LLC
Chambersburg PA
CBHW032135080426
42733CB00008B/1077